Spoonbill Swamp

For Mary, Ursa, and Zoe —M.L.
For Bill and Jason and those great exotic trips —B.Z.G.

Published by Henry Holt and Company, Inc.,
115 West 18th Street, New York, New York 10011.
Published simultaneously in Canada by Fitzhenry & Whiteside Ltd.,
195 Allstate Parkway, Markham, Ontario L3R 4T8.

Library of Congress Cataloging-in-Publication Data
Guiberson, Brenda Z.
Spoonbill swamp / Brenda Z. Guiberson ; illustrated by Megan Lloyd.
Summary: Depicts a swamp and the creatures that inhabit it,
focusing on the day-to-day activities of spoonbills and alligators.
1. Swamp fauna—Juvenile literature.   2. Spoonbills—Juvenile
literature.   3. Alligators—Juvenile literature.   [1. Swamp
animals.   2. Spoonbills.   3. Alligators.]   I. Lloyd, Megan, ill.   II. Title.
QL114.5.G85   1992
591.5′26325—dc20   91-8555

ISBN 0-8050-1583-3 (hardcover)
3   5   7   9   10   8   6   4   2
ISBN 0-8050-3385-8 (paperback)
3   5   7   9   10   8   6   4

First published in hardcover in 1992 by Henry Holt and Company, Inc.
First Owlet paperback edition, 1994

Printed in the United States of America
on acid-free paper. ∞

Spoonbill Swamp

Brenda Z. Guiberson
Illustrated by Megan Lloyd

Henry Holt and Company   New York

Cheep. Chirp, cheep. Three fluffy spoonbills bob up and down, up and down, high in a mangrove tree.

Cheep. Chirp, cheep. They tell their parents they are hungry again.

The father spoonbill flaps into the nest. He spreads his large wings to shade the chicks. He is their pink umbrella, protecting them from the glaring sun and the falcon that flies overhead.

This time, it is mother's turn to answer the hungry cries of the spoonbill chicks. *Hop. Flutter.* She moves to the top of the tree. With a great flapping of wings, she soars into the air, coloring the sky with crimson, pink, and orange.

Not far from this island rookery, a craggy-nosed alligator naps in the hot afternoon sun. Some baby alligators rest by her feet and some sleep on her huge scaly back. A zebra butterfly dances near them in the sunlight.

After a while, the craggy-nosed alligator gets too warm. She pushes up on thick, stubby legs until only the tip of her huge tail touches the ground. The tiny alligators crawl over and around one another as they slither down her sides to the muddy banks.

The mother alligator lifts four babies into her gaping mouth.
They peek around the pointed teeth.

Slowly, gently, the mother carries them across the spongy land. The other babies follow close behind.

Weaving high above the mangrove islands, the mother spoonbill flies over the alligators and two brown pelicans. She swoops above a family of otters and a great blue heron.

Finally the spoonbill zigzags down to a shallow cove to look for food. Minnows and sailfin mollies swim away from the splash.

Stretch. Bend. The spoonbill dips her beak into the water. Carefully she walks across the muddy bottom. She doesn't need to see into the still, murky water. The spoonbill feels for something to eat with her long , flat bill.

Snap. Trap. She finds a minnow supper and sends it down her long throat. *Swish, swirl,* back and forth, she feels for more. The wading bird collects shrimp, back swimmers, and small fish to bring to her baby chicks.

On the other side of the swamp, the craggy-nosed alligator puts her babies down in tall marsh grass. All the tiny alligators crawl into this shady spot, and the mother nudges them close together. They can hardly be seen. Their black-and-yellow bands of color blend into the shadows.

Soon the baby alligators fall asleep in the shade.

While her babies nap, the mother slides quietly into the water. She uses her short webbed feet to paddle and keep her balance as she swims away to look for food.

Splosh. Splish. She swims around a long row of crisscrossed roots and turns into a shallow cove. She sinks into a carpet of floating duckweed. Only two round eyes and a wide craggy nose stay above the water.

The mother spoonbill splashes nearby under thick mangrove branches. *Swish, swirl,* she searches for food one last time.

Suddenly the bird stops. She sees whirlpools and ripples in the duckweed. The water shimmers as something moves. It looks like a log, but it is not. Two glistening eyes stare out from the shadows.

Flutter. Splash. The huge alligator raises its tail as the spoonbill skims across the water. The hungry reptile lunges forward with her mouth open wide.

Snap.

The mouth closes on a gulp of warm air and
a fluffy pink feather left behind.

Flapflapflap. The spoonbill flies off to the safety of an ancient tree. She spreads her wings to dry and rests in the glow of the sinking sun. She looks out across the watery gulf when a woodpecker rattles the tree limb. The sky is now the color of the spoonbill.

Ee-yurk. Ee-yurk, yurk. In the swamp below, the craggy-nosed alligator hears her babies cry. With a loud *hissss,* she turns in the water. Her powerful tail churns the water as she rushes back to the marsh grasses and charges up to the land. She hisses again as a raccoon skitters away from the frightened baby alligators.

The alligators eat insects and small fish close to shore. Then, in the last rays of the orange sun, the mother alligator leads a crooked line of babies across the land to her water hole. Months ago, she dug this hole with powerful sweeps of her tail. Now it is full of water and protected by a thick growth of cattails and water lilies. The alligators slip into the warm water and stay all night.

Above them, the mother bird joins a gathering flock, sweeping low, soaring high, on a homeward flight to the mangrove island. The rookery is filled with nests, some with eggs and some with chicks. Mother knows which is hers.

Cheep. Chirp, cheep. Three fluffy spoonbills wait with open mouths. Father flutters up to a high branch and mother comes into the nest. She coughs up the food in her stomach and the chicks reach into her throat to eat. *Cheep, cheep. CHEEP.* Everyone wants a turn.

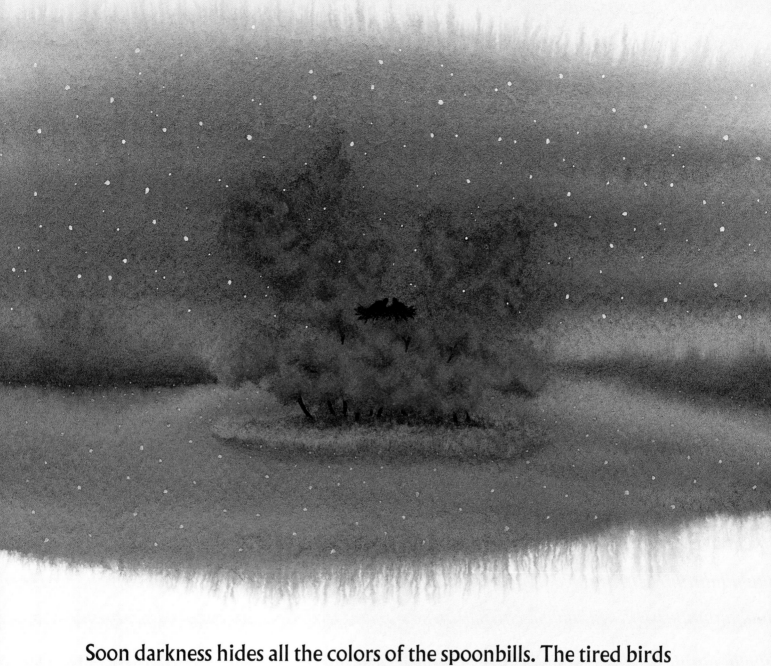

Soon darkness hides all the colors of the spoonbills. The tired birds tuck their wings and sleep. Crickets fill the night air with chirping. A bullfrog croaks from somewhere below.

Then, *cheep. Chirp, cheep.* The sun is up and the birds in the nest are hungry again. It is father's turn to fly to the shallow waters. Mother spreads her wings to be the pink umbrella.

Not far away, the alligators rest on a tangle of grass. The mother lifts her tail into the first sunlight that reaches over the trees. Because she and the babies are cold, they move slowly and are not hungry at all. They wait for the morning sun to warm them. It is the beginning of a new day in the swamp.

BIRD AND THE BEAST

The American alligator will never fly, but it does have a few things in common with the roseate spoonbill. They both build nests, lay eggs and protect them, then watch over the babies and respond to their cries. The spoonbills do this as a pair, but the female alligator handles these responsibilities alone.

Both the alligator and the spoonbill have special abilities to help them in their search for food. The spoonbill has sensitive nerve endings in its bill that allow it to find food by feel. An alligator has taste buds on the side of its mouth and feeds by sweeping the head from side to side. It can continually grow new teeth to replace ones that are lost. The alligator also has a third eyelid, thin and transparent, that closes when it swims. This extra lid is like a skin diver's mask and helps it to see better underwater.

The spoonbill and alligator are both finicky about temperatures. They like it warm. The alligator, which is cold-blooded, will not eat if it is too cold and can go weeks or months without a meal. The warm-blooded spoonbill, however, needs to eat all the time.

Both of these creatures have been heavily hunted for the fashion market. Spoonbill feathers were very popular at the turn of the century as decorations for hats. The bird almost disappeared until laws were enacted to protect it. The alligator, too, was in jeopardy, because its soft underside makes fancy shoes, purses, and belts. Other laws were passed for the protection of the alligator. Now the main danger to this bird and beast is the destruction of their environment. New construction, irrigation projects, and pollution continually threaten the habitat of the swamp.